of humankind

# of humankind peter lavery

With a Foreword by Robin Muir

KRUSE

For Kimberley

foreword by robin muir

That Peter Lavery is well known to us as an advertising photo-grapher, given the anonymity under which even the most sparkling of the discipline's practitioners works, is something of an achievement. Rarely are they accredited to or identified with the pictures they assiduously make. Without wishing to depreciate or underappreciate the sheer hard work that goes into an advertising assignment, I am reminded of the great American curator John Szarkowski, who once wrote about all the triumphs - acknowledged or not - of those photographers who are 'mercenaries during the week, [doing] their best work on week-ends.' Lavery's day job has given him the means to travel the world, and here, laid out on these pages, are the extraordinary side-effects that work has brought him and now brings us.

Lavery has had a concomitant career as a documentary photographer, most prominently for the *Observer Magazine*, and perhaps it is for this work and its most recent mani-festation that he is known to a still larger audience. Lavery's

portfolio *Circus Work*, published as a book in 1997 and shown fittingly as a travelling show, surveys - much as its title suggests - a way of life that is threatening to disappear as the new century unfolds. Recently I saw one photograph from the series in a collection put together for a private individual by Bruce Bernard. The picture shows Caroline Gebera, an equestrienne and trick rider in Ireland. It is a platinum print and excellent. Almost painterly in rendering, the photograph is reminiscent of the great Pictorialist tradition - that gasp of mid-Victorianism that unwittingly placed photography as an adjunct to painting rather than as the distinct art it would eventually become. Bernard, a picture editor and art historian, disdained for years to consider photography an 'art' or to write about it with anything like the flowing grace with which he wrote about painting. When he finally did, his measured elegance and unostentatious enthusiasm proved that, beyond any doubt, photography *was* an art.

Bruce wrote the foreword to Lavery's book of circus photographs. He did not suffer fools gladly. (In fact, said one friend ruefully, 'He didn't suffer *anyone* gladly.') Even when in admiration, he was a stranger to hyperbole and a master of restraint. On a handful of occasions the restraint was loosened a little. He said this about Lavery's work: 'These pictures, I believe, show Peter Lavery to be a photographer of the first rank in his human and pictorial perception and his undoubted technical skill.' Later, he told *The Independent* that 'it would take a really great photographer, perhaps an André Kertész, to equal or surpass what Lavery has done.' This is praise indeed. We cannot know the words he would have said in response to a glance through this, Lavery's second book of photographs. He would, I am sure - as do I - have found these pictures, taken by one who knows his photographic history better than many of his peers, not only redolent with understated echoes of the past but also generous in revealing and exploring it. The sensibility of Frederick Evans, champion of the platinum print, is here (a print of Evans's 'Sea of Steps' is for Lavery totemic; 'The whites were ethereal and the blacks went on for ever,' he says). Here too are the impartial scrutiny of August Sander, taxonomist of the German people, and the determination and sensitivity of Edward Curtis. Also, pervading all the pictures in this book is that sense of wonderment surely experienced by those pioneering travellers who first brought back haunting documents from far-off places. Lavery's portraits of Huli warriors, the Xingu tribesmen, the geisha, and the familiar punk musician remind us of Cartier-Bresson's remark that photographers deal in things which are continually vanishing and which no contrivance on earth can bring back.

To the early viewer of photographs, tilting perhaps a print up to the light, photography was a means to seize upon glimpses of the world. The play of light upon sensitized paper exposed landscapes, architectures, and ways of life that to the Victorian imagination remained half a lifetime away and as unfathomable as photographing the stars and planets. These documents were for the armchair traveller extraordinary vicarious experiences, tangible pieces of visual information, the first real links in the age of Darwinism to distant cultures. And when their scientific content was scrutinized and exhausted, they were marvelled at too, for frequently they were objects of remarkable beauty. Not for everyone did photography, as it did for the painter Daumier, 'describe everything and explain nothing'. As historian John Pultz has succinctly put it, at the dawn of the medium of photography

art and report were not distinct. In harmony with the artistic conventions of their time, nineteenth-century photographers sought to find sublime and picturesque beauty in the close observation of nature; they did not oppose aesthetics and the natural world but found the source for art in nature.

Victorian sensibilities were gripped by a fever for collecting both topographical and ethnographical likenesses of foreign lands. Commercial photographers were quick to make available such landscapes and portraits (or, better still, a portrait set in an appropriate landscape) and worked efficiently to satiate the public demand for visual possessions and its curiosity for information. In 1855, it was recommended that British cadets serving in India be given rudimentary instruction in the new photographic discipline - barely a decade and a half after its discovery. The war photographer Felice ('Felix') Beato turned from martial to topographic concerns. Though the pursuit of armed combat would still be his motive for travel, his landscapes of the Near and Far East without the accoutrements of war were souvenirs with a ready market in departing soldiers.

Of all the far-flung outposts of the Empire, India provided the richest ethnographical portraits of all, and the achievements of British photographers there are surveys as rich in variety as they are in intensity and depth. Linnaeus Tripe, an army captain, and the camera artists Samuel Bourne and Francis Frith - without compromising their visual flair - turned the documentation of the subcontinent into a concern of startling productivity. Frith's company was by far the largest photographic publisher of his day, bringing out with increasing regularity souvenirs in the form of postcards, cartes-de-visite, and larger-scale prints from places that its audience could never hope to reach and who yearned for more than the line drawings of an encyclopaedia could ever impart. Thus Frith's pictures are the most typical of the nineteenth-century genre photograph. The subject is invariably positioned frontally (no suggestion of the observational here), with clear emphasis on detail - tools, weaponry, clothing, and the embellishments of attire. The backdrop, a tribal hut perhaps or a market or meeting place, contributes a little more about the culture and surroundings of the sitter.

Peter Lavery has chosen, like the best of the pioneering Victorians, to make his portraits much more than just likenesses and, following their example in part, has frequently elected to carry out the process on a large-format plate camera. Lartigue greeted his first plate camera at the age of seven with the words, 'It's enormous - like an ogre!' and although it must be cumbersome on an ice floe with an Inuit hunter Lavery clearly wields it with dexterity. Occasionally his plate camera allows him to put on more of an act for his sitters than he wants from them in return. He said recently that

Part of my habit of picture-taking is to attempt not to direct or instruct so much as to try to capture that first aspect of a person. It's not just about an expression - it might be a way you've seen somebody leaning, standing, or something else. And there's often a way of being able to bring that out with the *5 x 4 or allowing it just to happen. You're also communicating with people much better. They are not so intimidated. They find it amusing. Even the Xingu know what a camera is - it's something small that clicks, not this large thing.*

Lavery acknowledges the inevitability of creeping Occidentalism - like Irving Penn, who found that those he had photographed with bows and arrows, spears and blowpipes were only a few years later walking around in 'ready-made suits, armed with briefcases'.

The plain black backdrop brings to mind an itinerant photographer of the Edwardian age, a *saloniste* without a salon, but the edges betray the intrusion of real life - the tyre of a Land Rover, a stray arm cradling a ukulele, a cherry-blossom garden. 'I didn't want people to look like ornaments,' explains Lavery. 'Equally, I don't want to take over their spirit and make them work in my own way.' Set up at various vantage points, occasionally the backcloth becomes the focus of community life for half an hour. 'I like the idea of people going about their business and suddenly they are in front of a camera.' The impression that lasts is that Lavery's subjects could have stayed that way for a considerable time, enraptured by the process and the performance.

Peter Lavery's photographs are not what one might expect as anthropological documents. Not in the sense that, say, a museum might once have expected its intrepid ambassadors to send back specimens of wild flowers or insects pickled in formaldehyde. Lavery's photographs are not exercises in the recording of tribes. He hasn't given us details to differentiate one from the other, no catalogue of jewellery, weaponry, or masks, nor has he listed their idiosyncracies and similarities or contrasted his modern-day Caucasians with their counterparts in the rain forests of New Guinea or on ice-bound wastes at the top of the world. Rather, as he has said before, 'I am in agreement with those artists who hold that the human heart is seen through the face' and, further, that he tries 'to make the pictures work wherever we are and they are. You can't go there, take somebody by the arm, and set it all up. You just take away any spirit they might have.'

There can surely be no finer and more dignified tribute to a book of ethnographic portraits than that of George Horse Capture, a native American of Montana, who wrote of Edward Curtis's *North American Indian* - not the twenty-volume life work but the recent abridgement *Native Nations* - that 'As I near the end of my journey, the sun is bright, flooding the world with warmth and light. Blossoms are everywhere. It is a great honor to be asked to write this introduction...' He continues, 'I will present fifty copies of this book to fifty Indian high schools and colleges. Several full-page, loose-leaf, unbound tribal portraits will accompany them', and he ends by wishing the publisher of the venture - and by inference the shade of the photographer too, who died unremembered - that they all 'walk in sunshine'. No one who looks through the present book, perhaps the first of a series (though not, I gather, of twenty volumes), I am sure would wish Peter Lavery and his sitters from distant lands and nearer to home anything remotely less.

Cocking, West Sussex , June 2000

of humankind

Brazil, September 1988

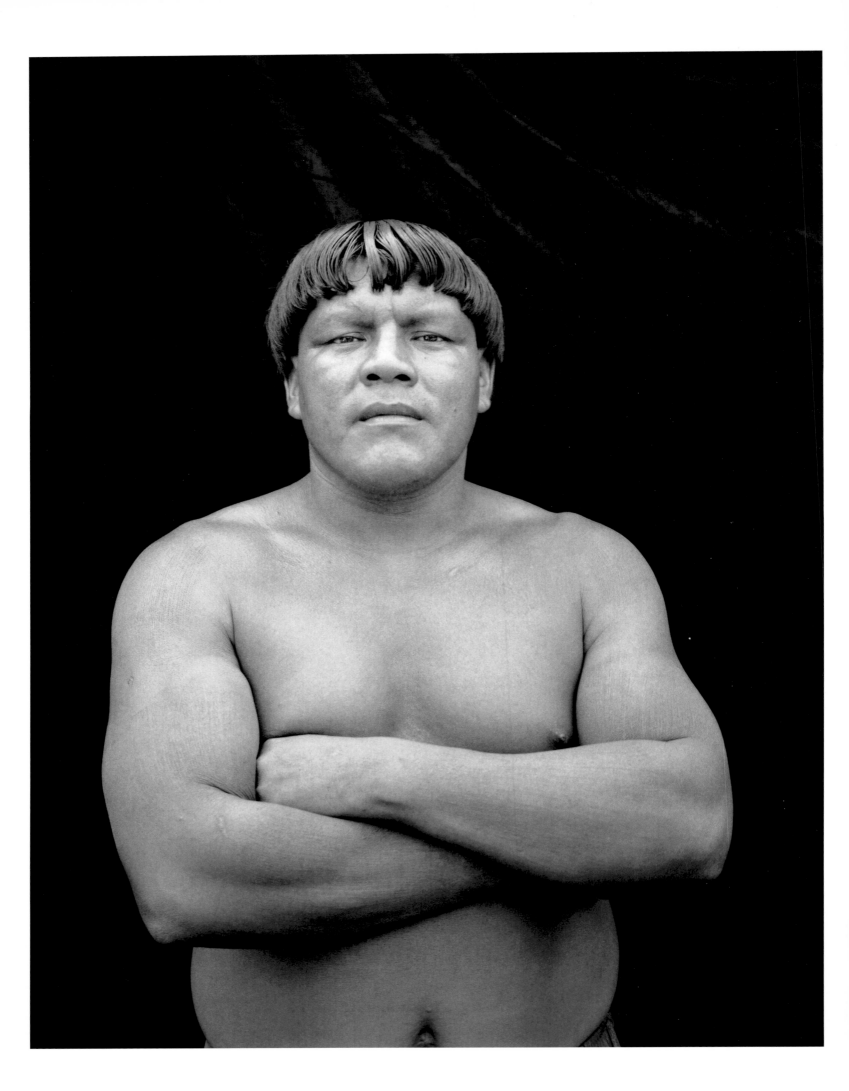

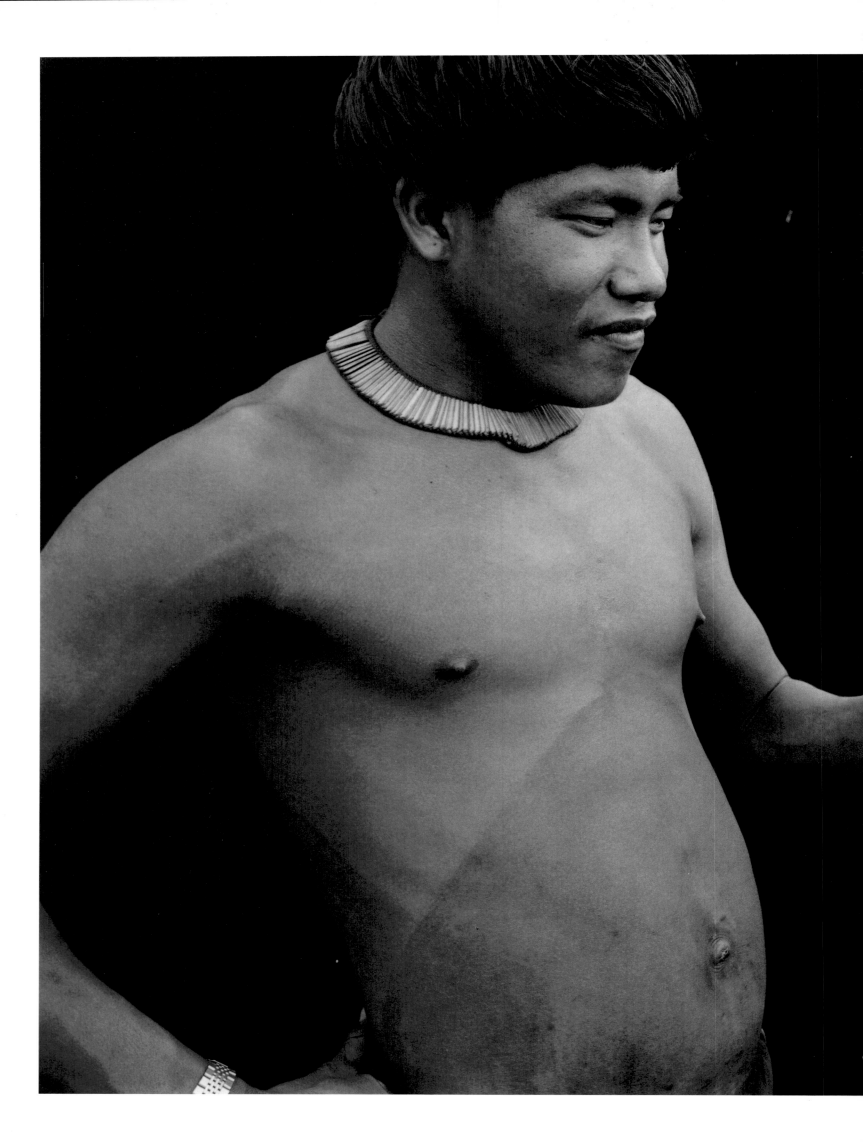

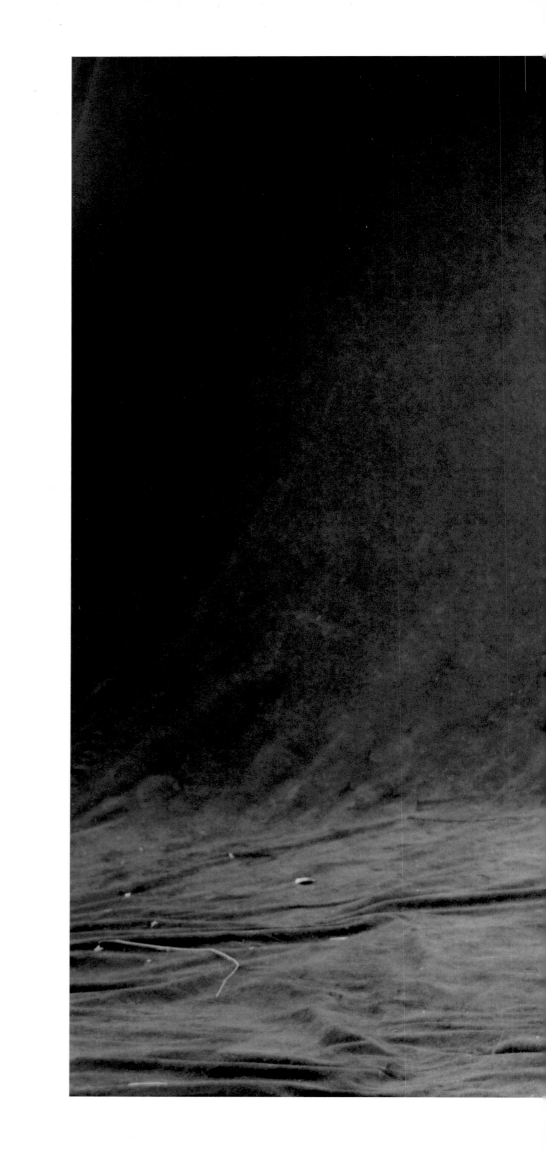

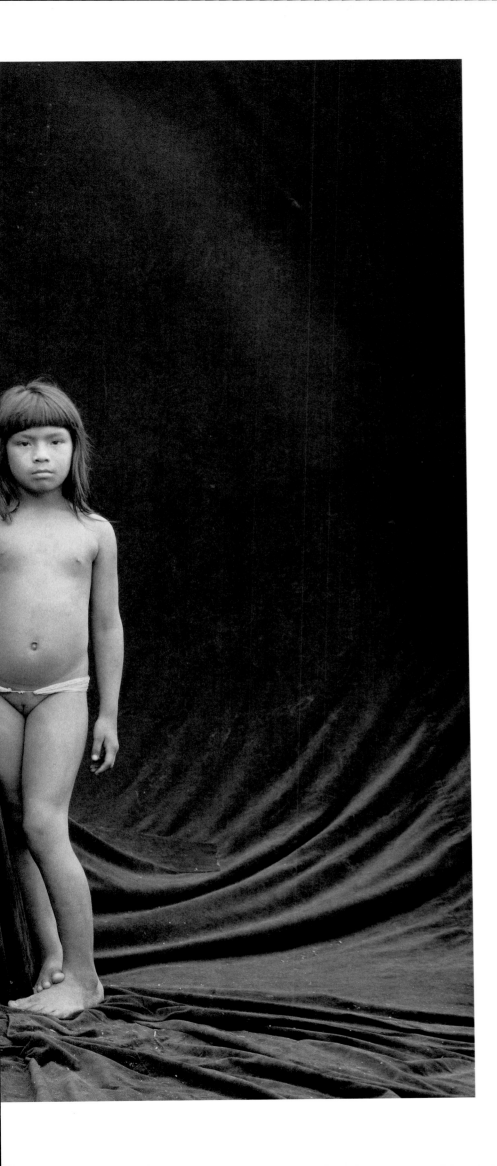

Cannes, June 1992

Alice Springs, August 1991

Kenya, July 1991

Greenland, July 1991

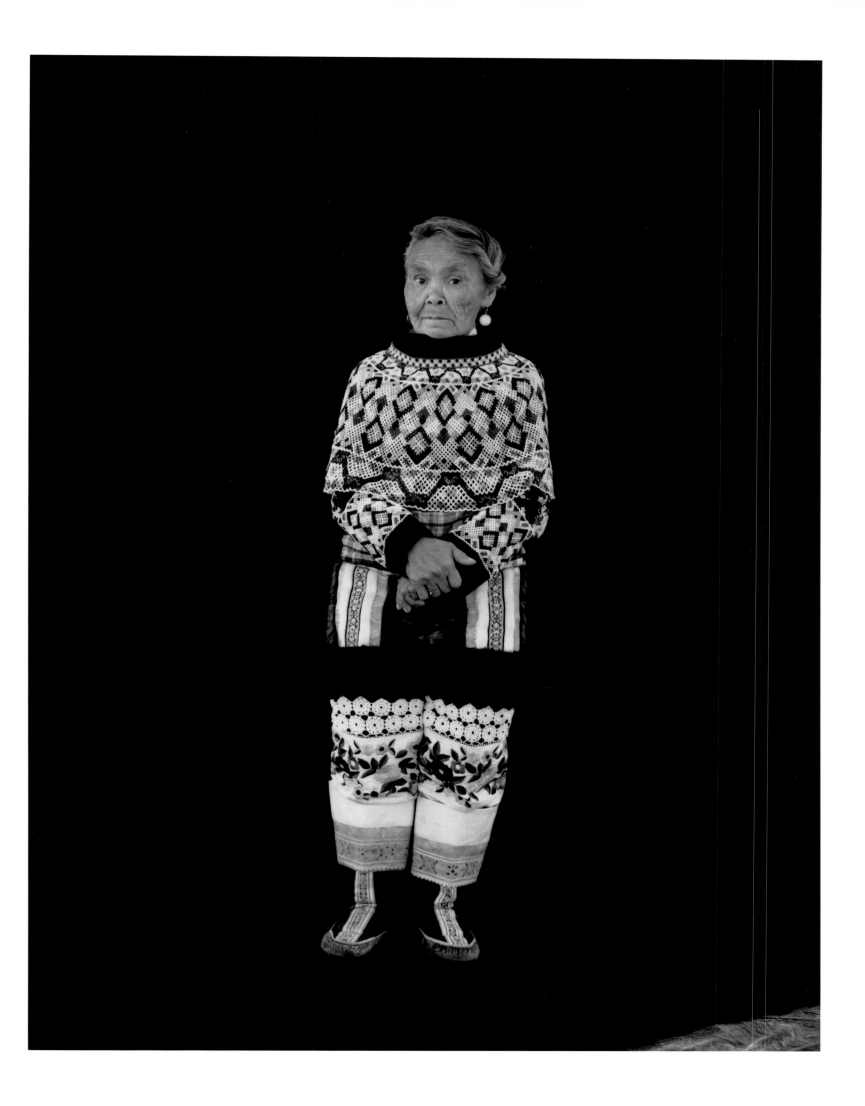

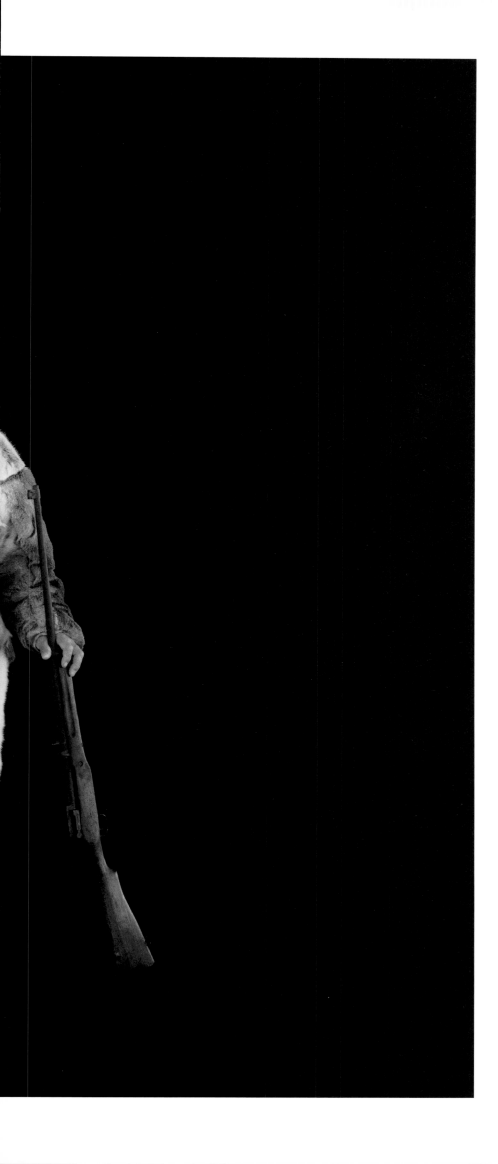

Nevada, October 1993

Los Angeles, October 1993

San Francisco, October 1993

Tunisia, February 1996

Las Vegas, October 1993

New Mexico, August 1992

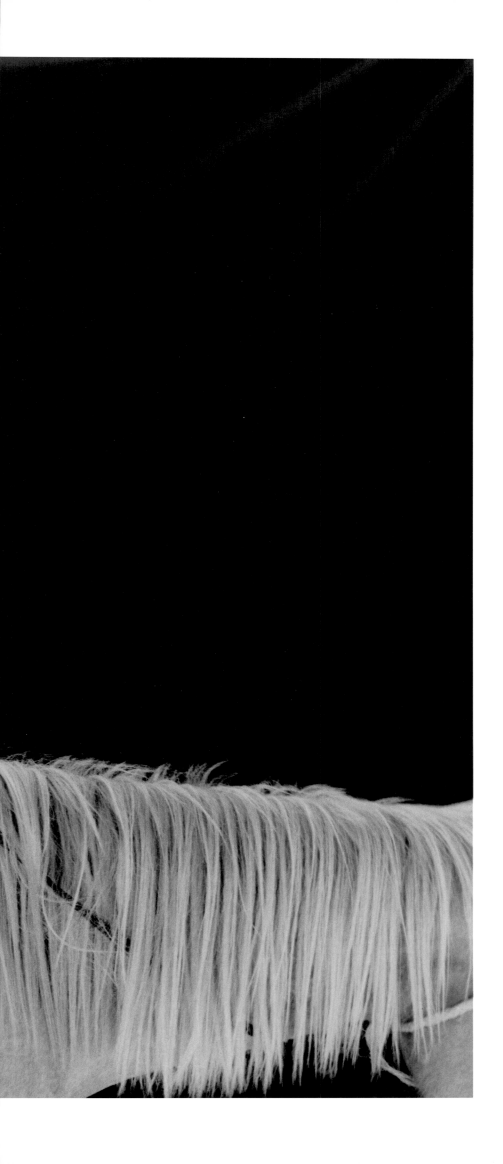

New Mexico, October 1992

Poona, February 1989

Papua New Guinea, November 1991

Oxfordshire, July 1997

Wiltshire, September 1999

Yorkshire, October 1995

Capetown, May 1996

China, June 1991

Buenos Aires, February 1988

Oman, December 1999

Kyoto, March 2000

my portraits peter lavery

Years ago, soon after I left the Royal College of Art, I acquired a two-volume set of *Women of All Nations*, a kind of anthropological survey of world-wide types and customs. The book was generously endowed with exotic photographs of tribeswomen from every corner of the globe. Revisited today, such a publication - a memento of worlds that have by and large disappeared - is a mere curiosity and probably scientifically suspect as well. Yet something about the variety and scope of the people portrayed caught my fancy. One day, I naively dreamed, I might be in a position to take advantage of any travels that photographic assignments brought my way and make portraits for myself of people in foreign lands who interested me. By the time the opportunity came - and, as important, a necessary awareness that the moment had arrived - I had been taking pictures of people of note all over Britain and abroad, both celebrities and ordinary folk elevated to the pages of the Sunday colour supplements of newspapers like *The Times* or *Telegraph* or *Observer*. The experience of this work in due course guided me in my approach to making the portraits presented in this book. But there was one big difference. I was now free (and eager) to photograph people who were not the object of editorial curiosity.

In 1988, a project concerning the rain forests of Brazil coupled with the interest of the *Observer Magazine* took me to the remote Yawalapiti tribe of the upper Xingu River, in Brazil. Here I planned to bring together various strands of my earlier experience of making portraits. I went to the rain forest with a piece of black velvet cloth, thick, heavy, and some twenty feet square. I knew that I wanted to play down the exoticism of my subjects. I knew that I was interested in the being under the body paint or feathers and primitive weapons. I was not going to be sidetracked by the trappings but was out to capture the simple and essential human character that lay under the strange, colourful exterior. Wanting my sitters to be believable as people, I was not going to ennoble them or to dictate to them their expressions. As much as possible, I wanted to keep myself, the photographer, out of the picture. Simply said but not easy to do. The use of a cloth backdrop, of course, is as old as photography itself.

The portraits in this book treat the human face and what is in it as the sole issue. From the start, I try to isolate the person being photographed from any competing background that will distract the viewer's eye. At the same time, to keep the sitter at ease (thereby allowing him or her to reveal everyday moods and emotions), I held my subjects as close to their surroundings as possible. In Brazil, my black background was many times hung by the very doorways of the tribesmen's thatched huts. In Greenland, amongst the Inuit hunters, I draped my cloth over the nearest ice outcrop. In each case, the sitter was not on my territory but on his own. In the finished picture we may see him against a neutral background, but for his part he is looking out on his immediate, everyday world.

The longer I take to make a picture the more I lose my subject - that is, lose the unguarded look that he or she first offered me. Therefore I try to keep contact with my sitters brief. It is always daunting to see the quality one is trying to capture in a face drift away or completely change. From a possible five to twenty exposures, it often turns out that my initial picture is the one I ultimately use.

The photographs chosen for this book are highly selective. As will be readily apparent - and contrary to the possible expectation of geographical representativeness hinted at by my title, *Of Humankind* - there is no aim here to set forth artificial symmetries. Therefore nothing should be adduced from the fact that I have presented some twelve or so portraits of Brazilian tribesmen but from cultures closer to our own - those of a Frenchwoman on a Cannes beach or a young white Capetown student of ballet - only two photographs. My in-

terest has always been in individuals, not types. My aim has not been sociological documentation but the production of an artistic object, the photograph. In the end, the quality of the photograph as a photograph, an individual object, has been my sole criterion for inclusion or exclusion. Whole series of pictures - of Irish ghillies, of French waiters, of Italian farmers - I found ultimately wanting in some element and so have kept out of the current choice.

On rereading these paragraphs, I am reminded how close to an obsession has been my concern with keeping myself out of the portraits I make. And yet only the other day someone who knows my work well and is also aware of my abiding aesthetic precept remarked after studying a number of my photographs in succession that she recognized little bits of me, certain traits or quirks, in them. Have I come short of my ideal, then? I hope not. Still, the observation - no doubt kindly meant and in no way a damning criticism - brings to mind those lapidary words of Jorge Luis Borges, who noted that
A man sets himself the task of depicting the world. Year after year, he fills a space with images of provinces, kingdoms, mountains, bays, ships, islands, fishes, rooms, instruments, stars, horses, and people. Just before he dies, he discovers that out of this patient labyrinth of lines emerge the features of his own face.

I ponder this revelation; it makes me uneasy but perhaps the import is salutary. There is a mystery in all art that is beyond us fully to direct or control. Knowing this, I am cheered.

Minety, Wiltshire, May 2000

notes and captions

Photographers have different views about captioning their pictures. Purists among us want the image to tell the whole story without recourse to words of elucidation or explanation. I confess that I myself tend to this point of view, yet I do appreciate that readers want and often need some orientation. Opposite the photographs in this book I have provided the barest possible information - the broadest general location where a picture was taken and the date. More information, picture by picture, is given here in these pages. But even at this point, I have been stinting. However, in flagrant contradiction of such parsimony, I include below some notes and reminiscences.

The Xingu

The Xingu tribes are found in the vast remote heartland of the Brazilian rain forest, in an 8,500 square-mile national pre-

serve created some forty years ago to shield the indigenous population from disastrous contacts with outsiders. Here, in an area half the size of Switzerland, live sixteen tribes, each speaking a different language, in an environment where they are able to continue their traditions with limited interference from the modern world.

The Yawalapiti, the people whose village I visited, numbered around 180 at the time of my stay; in the 1960s they were fewer than thirty. When I arrived, it was my good fortune to find Sandra Wellington there. A British woman, she had been working with the Xingu and living among them for a decade. Through her, we got close to Aritana, the Yawalapiti's young chief, who later dictated to Sandra the succinct and profound remarks about the tribe's code of ethics that were to accompany some of these Xingu photographs in the *Observer Magazine*.

Our arrival in the village happened to coincide with the tribes' important Kuarup festival, which honours a chief who has died in the previous year. Before and after the funeral rites, there are intertribal wrestling and spear-throwing contests. The wrestlers' hair is coloured blood-red with a sticky dye that is mixed with an oil to give it a glossy sheen. Geometric designs derived from nature - representing various local fauna such as raptors, wildfowl, otters, monkeys, pumas, and armadillos - are applied to their skin using the blue-black juice of the fruit of the genipap tree. The Xingu believe that tight bands worn around the men's ankles and arms increase their strength. Champion wrestlers, who earn great respect, like to wear feather headdresses or shell necklaces about their waists to show they have no fear of being thrown.

Fish is the mainstay of the Xingu diet, together with the manioc root, which is ground into a flour and baked into large pancakes or else is made into a gruel with water. Once a year, the elders gather for a ceremony conducted by the village shaman in Aritana's thatched house, where the shaman produces three herbal 'cigars' that he has rolled himself from various forest plants. The chief takes his place in the middle of about a dozen men, who sit in a circle blowing smoke into his face. Each cigar is smoked in turn during the course of several hours. The meeting, aided and enhanced by the smoke, is held to discuss the tribe's future. The first cigar stimulates the imagination; the second helps turn creative ideas into concrete suggestions; and the third helps consolidate general ideas and convert them into practical policy. I myself sat at Aritana's one night and was treated to one of these 'cigars', which indeed was stimulating.

The dignity and simplicity of the Yawalapiti is impressive. Sandra Wellington has pointed out that it was thanks to the life work of the famed Villas-Boas brothers, who kept missionaries out of the area after the previously unknown tribes of the Xingu were discovered in 1943, that their beliefs and customs have survived largely intact. Aritana has said of his people that

The special beauty of our lives here is that we still live in the same way as we always have, with the same legends, festivals, and beliefs of our ancestors, unlike so many other tribes who have, for one reason or another, put aside their old ways of life. Everyone is the same here - we have no rich or poor. We make most of the things we need ourselves and what we don't make we trade with neighbouring tribes. We don't like to fight or quarrel - why should we? What purpose does it serve? We prefer to live in peace in our villages and on friendly terms with everyone. This is why I call this land of ours Paradise.

The Masai

My first glimpse of the Masai was in the distance through the shimmering heat of mid-morning across a dry plain, with fabled Kilimanjaro in the background. Two herdsmen were driving a dozen cattle to water. What struck me was the sudden speck of intense red of their togas and their ochre-daubed bodies, which, in the monochrome of the dusty landscape, were a flash of life. Up close, they were impressive - tall, handsome, and proud. Their diet consisted of milk, meat, and blood. When at rest, they stood stork-like on one leg, leaning on a stick or on their javelin-like spears. I teamed up with a group of them, whom I met each morning and walked out with onto the plain to find a set of rocks or trees on which to drape my cloth, since their own mud huts were too low for this.

Lion-hunting, I came to find out, had once played an important part in the lives of the young warriors but was now proscribed. One of the men I photographed described a hunt from which he still bore a scar on his chest. A given number of warriors had tracked down a marauding lion, loosely encircling and driving it towards a single man, who made himself conspicuous so as to attract the animal. If the advancing lion can be hit by the spears of the other men, who have slowly closed in from the sides, all to the good; if not, the lone warrior is expected to take the full brunt of the lion's surge. Crouching, he plants the butt of his spear into the ground to one side of him and waits for the lion to leap and impale itself. Such a display of bravery gave a warrior special distinction among his fellow tribesmen, and, in the old days, allowed him to wear the *olewaru*, a headdress made from the lion's mane.

The Inuit

Sometimes in my travels sheer remoteness intrigued me. I suppose the central highlands of Papua New Guinea were physically, or geographically, the remotest spot I have yet taken pictures. But the place that *felt* most remote was Umanak, on the west coast of Greenland, 1,300 or so miles from the North Pole. Here I found people living alone or in small communities that were a three- or four-hour boat ride from the town.

They still eked out an existence by fishing and by hunting seal and narwhal. Their kayaks were hand-made of sealskin; their clothes, of seal, dog, polar bear, and reindeer. The world around them was incredibly hostile, hard, extreme, but in summer both the light and the blueness of the ice was intense and beautiful. Around the edges of Umanak and outlying communities one was immediately struck by the washing lines of drying fish. They stank, as did the ubiquitous dog shit that emerged from the snow in the spring thaw. The barking of dogs, which outnumbered people by far, was constant. Dogsleds were the main means of overland travel.

The constant threat to life that lurked in the harsh environment was apparent everywhere - crevices in the ice, crumbling icebergs, water you couldn't survive in for more than a minute or two. The place was pointed out to us where a taxi driver, usually safe in winter driving over the frozen sea, misjudged the extent of a thaw and went down behind the wheel. At the Umanak heliport coffins were stacked waiting for the ground to unfreeze enough for burials. But the seabed, glimpsed through crystalline water, served as a cemetery for cars and old refrigerators.

Papua New Guinea

There was some sort of small war on - I had been warned about it - when we arrived at the burnt-out huts in a clearing that was marked on the map as Margarima. The place was not a village or even a hamlet. The remains of a couple of hovels were smouldering, which made my driver want to keep his footdown and rush straight through. But the sight of a few warriors in a doorway and the sound of others cheering and shouting prompted me to have the driver stop. We had been on the road for six hours, and I was getting anxious to take some pictures.

In the darkness of one standing hut I could make out some thirty or forty armed men drinking, while a couple of others, using their spears as cues, were bent over a scruffy pool table that had no cloth. The windowless room was dark, and there was a rank smell of sweat. The whole lot seethed with anger. I learned that the fracas had something to do with a neighbouring village's cow and that someone had been killed. The fighting had stopped the day before.

Trying to organize some photographs, I set up my black velvet behind the hut. The driver and two bodyguards negotiated a fee, but after three or four pictures I could sense growing belligerence and thought it wise to retire and move on. As we threw the cloth into our Land Rover, a group of older warriors in feather headdresses arrived and insisted on having their pictures taken too. They seemed proud of the fighting kit they were rigged out in. I was reluctant but got my companions to hold the cloth in their hands from the back of our vehicle.

Again I worked quickly, but just as we were preparing to leave one of the locals - they were all armed with bows and arrows and spears, and many carried machetes - reached in and seized my cable release.

An eruption seemed imminent. I shouted to one of my men to produce some money and for a moment thought he was going to draw his gun instead. By now the Land Rover was surrounded by angry tribesmen with poised spears. Money was exchanged, I grabbed the cable, and we sped off. Turning to the man behind me, I saw glazed eyes and a mouth stained red with the fresh juice of betel nuts. It was a comic note.

Hours later, after endless bumping and jolting, with needles of blinding light shooting down through the forest canopy, the incident melted back into unreality. The impression one had in these highlands was of apprehension, of not knowing what was coming next. New Guinea was beautiful but raw. Or was it beautiful because it was raw?

China

In the countryside north of Guilin, in western Guangxi Province, no foreigners were to be seen, which made us an instant attraction when we set up our backdrop against a village schoolhouse. This was an area of China noted for its diverse minority ethnic groups - nationalities, the Chinese call them - the Bai, the Dong, the Zhuang, the Miao, and so forth. (Some of these minorities were readily told apart by their physical appearance, some by their dress, and of course there was considerable overlapping.) Peeping over the black cloth in a few of my portraits are the eight characters in Chinese script that it occurred to me only the other day to have translated. They turned out to be a slogan, or political directive, that reads: 'Education is the basis of our strategy for the next hundred years'. There was a holiday atmosphere about the place and a good deal of jollity as the villagers watched me and my plate camera.

Surprisingly, there was none of the shyness I had expected. The whole population, it seemed, was quite prepared to stop its normal activity and be photographed. After a few days in our Guilin hotel - used only by Chinese - we grew tired of the food, a sort of bland hotel version of national dishes rather than something typical of the area. I figure that if you want fresh food it's often safer to choose something that is still alive. I told my assistant that I had seen what looked like a pet shop but was sure was a restaurant. Off we went to it with our guide. By the entrance was a range of cages and tanks. We chose our meal by pointing to a rabbit, what appeared to be a guinea pig, a fish, and then a snake. The cage of songbirds we gave a miss. Next we settled back with beers and waited. In due course, a small glass of a red liquid arrived, and we were told it was good for our virility. I declined it. The guide quaffed it down. It was the snake's blood. The food was simple and delicious but not enough for the three of us. Wanting to improve my sign language, I thought to ask for another course without our guide's assistance and gave my best version of a quacking duck. Immediately, the proprietor-cook chuckled to communicate his perfect understanding. After some time, the *pièce de résistance* arrived - a large steaming bowl containing a jumble of fleshy green bits. Eventually, it dawned on us that we were staring into a bowl brimful of dismembered frogs.

We did not try again for the duck. In Guilin, we were befriended by a number of university students, who on several occasions took us around the town on their bicycles, discussed politics with us, and introduced us to the local snails, which were as big as your fist. There were few cars in Guilin at the time, but the number and rush of bicycles bordered on the lethal. The airport was unrelieved chaos, yet I loved China - or, rather, this single corner of it that I have seen.

Buenos Aires

Early 1988 found me crisscrossing Buenos Aires for three weeks, trying to make a photographic portrait of that vast and fascinating city. Quite by accident one night, driving along the Avenida General Paz, the highway that marks the perimeter of the city, I noticed an old car drawn up on the hard shoulder with two exotic (and scantily-dressed) girls standing there along with what appeared to be a couple of pimps. They were - and it seemed that the lot of them were busy picking up lorry drivers and motorists for a bit of quick sex. I stopped, took a couple of pictures, and made contact with the girls. Only they weren't girls but individuals in various stages of sexual transition.

A few days later, I photographed them under less pressing circumstances just outside the city in the little rural setting where a number of them lived communally in a small house down a leafy dirt track. Some were Uruguayans. They were all willing to have their pictures taken, almost as evidence of their hard-won allure, and eager to tell their stories.

One scrawny boy, still in the earliest stages of transformation, worked as a housemaid and sent remittances to his unwitting family in Uruguay. There was a certain poignancy about them - the risks and dangers they ran, the mutual aid they extended each other. Some were quite feminine and attractive; others, plainly gross. All shared the dream of one day being real women.

The Geisha

The world of the geisha, in its attempt to arrest time and keep an old tradition untainted, is endlessly fascinating. The stylized beauty of the women themselves, their strict codes of conduct, the infinite fine distinctions in their make-up and dress are unique or, put another way, quintessentially Japanese.

Trained as entertainers, the geisha masters such arts as etiquette, conversation, music, and classical dance. For my part, I knew little about them before I reached Kyoto, but I had a vague idea that they might give me something of the bearing they cultivate, something of the qualities demanded by their total dedication to their art and their ultimate mastery of refinement. I thought, in short, that the power of photography might reveal something of the mysterious essence of the geisha that is deeper than her surface beauty. In part the geisha's art is in her performance; but equally she gives off a dimension of spiritual unity in which, as I found out, she herself is her art.

Kyoto is acknowledged as the capital of the geisha, and the city has five recognized geisha communities. It was unusual that I was allowed to photograph these women behind the scenes while they dressed in private rooms, where their store of kimonos was held. I also took pictures back stage at the theatre where dances were performed for the annual cherry-blossom season.

The nuances of geisha dress are also full of fascination. The height at which the *obi*, the waist band, is tied, for example, carries connotations of chastity. A wife wears hers just below the breasts, young girls wear it covering their breasts entirely, while a geisha who intends to appear alluring and attractive to men will wear the *obi* much lower. Another element of the geisha is her chaste eroticism.

15 Yawalapiti tribesman

16 Aritana, chief of the Yawalapiti tribe

18 Mapulu, daughter of a Kamayura chieftain

19 Young Xingu mother and her children

20 Young Xingu with a pet macaw

23 Yawalapiti man with bow and arrow

24 Xingu tribesman

26 Xingu children

29 Xingu village shaman

30 Xingu wrestlers

33 Yawalapiti man with a speared fish

34 Aritana's sister, Tataruyap

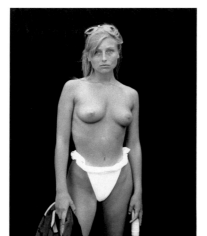

37 Girl on a french beach

39 Ringer with branding iron

40 Ringer and bull terrier

43 Australian cowhand

44 Masai warrior

46 Younger Masai hunters and herdsmen

48 Masai tribesmen

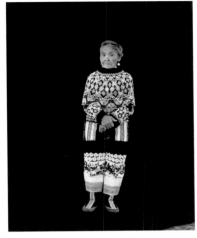

51 Inuit grandmother

52 Greenlander family

54 Inuit hunter

57 Nevada oilman

58 Motorcycle traffic policeman

61 California diner waitress

63 Tunisian goatherd

65 Navajo in feather headdress

66 Navajo woman

68 New Mexico horseman

70 Boy in festival costume

73 Girl in Navajo festival dress

75 Hindu woman

76 Girl with water pot

80 Huli men with drums

78 Huli tibesman with pipes

83 Unmarried Huli girl

84 Old Huli tribesman

85 Huli woman in mourning

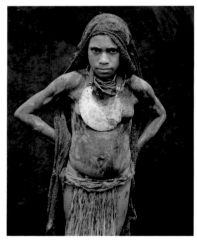

86 Mendi girl

89 Huli warrior

90 Warrior with cane spear and arrow

91 Warrior with headdress

92 Huli warriors

93 Old Huli warrior

95 Punk musician

96 Mary Lavery (1928-1999)

99 Pigeon fancier

100 Young ballerina

104 YAO women

103 Gulin men

107 Minority ethnic women from Guangxi

108 Guangxi ploughma

110 Mulam pipe smokers

112 River Plate trans-sexuals

115 Bedouin tribesman

117 Mahri women and children

118 Youth from Wadi Sham

119 Young Omani

121 Wadi Sham man with rushes

123 A maiko, or apprentice geisha

124 A geiko, or Kyoto geisha

125 Geikos

127 Maiko in her young woman's kimono

129 Geiko backstage at a dance theatre

acknowledgements

Scores of people, drivers, guides, interpreters, friends - some paid, some unpaid - helped in the realization of this project since its concrete beginning in 1988. I am especially grateful to Sandra Wellington for her assistance during my ten-day stay among the Xingu and to Aritana Yawalapiti, chief of his tribe, for his considered statements about Xingu life. These eventually found their way into the *Observer Magazine*, in June 1989, along with some of my portraits of his people. I wish to thank my friend June Stanier, then picture editor of the magazine, for her interest and support.

On numerous trips to the western United States I received the assistance of Larry Campbell. The Bureau of Indian Affairs of the U.S. Department of the Interior also helped with information and services. I am grateful to Raleigh International for its assistance during my stay in Oman; and especially to Kyoko and Graham Harris for their help in Japan while I photographed geishas.

The guiding spirit of my late friend Bruce Bernard I hope enriches these pages. Thanks are due to another old friend, Syd Shelton, who has always been available for assistance in problems of design and computer graphics.

The project, both in the field and in the studio, has received the benefits of my able assistants Tony Lumb, James Lampard, Jonathan Coffin and - in the early days - Richard McConnell, whom I thank. More than to anyone else, perhaps, I owe a debt to my wife Kimberley, who has relentlessly organized the myriad details of my journeys abroad, accompanied me on many of them, generally pushed and inspired me, and ultimately led the way in bringing this book to fruition.

Thanks also to Roy Snell and David Toms for their prints.

For final preparation of the text, I am grateful to Alex Leith for research; to Norman Thomas di Giovanni for editorial guidance and his translation of the words of Jorge Luis Borges quoted in my remarks about taking portraits; and to Robin Muir for his foreword.

P.L.

Also by Peter Lavery: *Circus Work* (1997)
ISBN 0-9529647-0-8

Published by Kruse Verlag, Hamburg, Germany.
Design by Artillery, Hamburg. Scans and reproduction by Reproduktion Onnen & Klein, Hamburg.
Printed by Druckerei Weidmann, Hamburg.

Kruse Verlag GmbH, Kampstr. 11, 20357 Hamburg, Germany. Phone: 0049 40 4328246-0. Fax: 0049 40 4328246-12.
E-mail: info@KrusePublishers.com Internet: www.KrusePublishers.com

Distribution in North, South and Central America, Asia, Australia and Africa by D.A.P./Distributed Art Publishers,
155 Sixth Avenue, 2nd floor, New York, N.Y. 10013. Phone: 001 212 6271999. Fax: 001 212 6279484.

Distribution in Europe, Asia, Australia and Africa by IDEA Books, Nieuwe Herengracht 11, 1011 RHK Amsterdam,
Netherlands. Fax: 0031 20 6209299. E-Mail: idea@ideabooks.nl

Distribution in Germany, Austria and Switzerland by Kruse Verlag.

First Kruse Verlag edition, 2000. Printed in Germany. ISBN 3-934923-02-X